J
951.95
Dav

Countries of the World

South Korea

by Lucile Davis

Consultant:
David A. Parker
Librarian/Information Associate
Korean Information Center, Embassy of the Republic of Korea

Bridgestone Books
an imprint of Capstone Press
Mankato, Minnesota

Bridgestone Books are published by Capstone Press
818 North Willow Street, Mankato, Minnesota 56001
http://www.capstone-press.com

Library of Congress Cataloging-in-Publication Data
Davis, Lucile.
    South Korea/by Lucile Davis.
    p. cm.—(Countries of the world)
    Includes bibliographical references and index.
    Summary: A simple introduction to the geography, history, customs,
foods, language, and people of South Korea. Also includes instructions
for making a Korean mask.
    ISBN 0-7368-0070-0
    1. Korea (South)—Juvenile literature. [1. Korea (South)]
I. Title. II. Series: Countries of the world (Mankato, Minn.)
DS902.D28 1999   98-15910
951.95   CIP
                                        AC

Editorial Credits
Martha E. Hillman, editor; James Franklin, cover designer and illustrator;
  Sheri Gosewisch, photo researcher
Photo Credits
Embassy of Korea, 5 (bottom)
Gregory Cherin, 6
John Elk III, 16
Photo Researchers/Alain Evrard, 14
StockHaus Limited, 5, (top)
Thomas Ansel Price II, 10, 18
Visuals Unlimited/Charles Preitner, cover; Ken Lucas, 12
Wild Bill Melton, 8, 20

Table of Contents

Name: Republic of Korea

Capital: Seoul

Population: More than 45 million

Language: Korean

Religions: Buddhism, Christianity

Size: 38,375 square miles
(99,391 square kilometers)

South Korea is slightly larger than the U.S. state of Indiana.

Crops: Rice, soybeans, vegetables

Maps

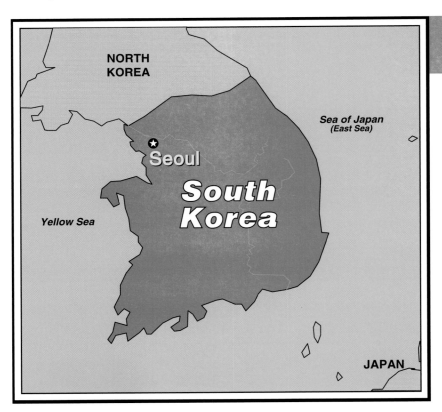

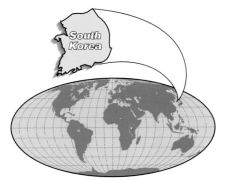

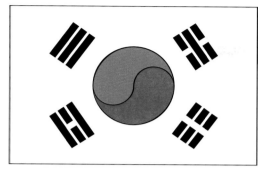

Flag

The flag of the Republic of Korea is white. A circle is in the center. The top of the circle is red. The bottom is blue. The circle is called t'aeguk (ta-GOOK). The t'aeguk stands for the universe in balance. Four black figures surround the circle. The figures represent heaven, earth, fire, and water. South Koreans call their flag T'aegukki (TA-goo-kee). T'aegukki shows that South Koreans are in balance with the universe.

Currency

The unit of currency in South Korea is the won. One hundred chun equal one won.

In the late 1990s, about 1,400 won equaled one U.S. dollar. About 1,000 won equaled one Canadian dollar.

The Land of South Korea

South Korea is on the Korean Peninsula. This area of land is surrounded by water on three sides. The Korean Peninsula reaches south from the east coast of Asia.

South Korea covers the southern part of the peninsula. North Korea covers the northern part. South Korea and North Korea used to be one country called Korea. But different groups of people wanted different kinds of government. Korea became two countries.

Mountains and forests cover much of South Korea. Low, flat land lies along the southern and western coasts.

Monsoons sometimes blow across South Korea. A monsoon is a strong wind. Monsoons bring wet weather during summer. They bring dry weather during winter.

Mountains and forests cover much of South Korea.

Life at Home

South Koreans follow many traditions in their homes. They have practiced these traditions for many years. People sit on the floor at small tables to eat. They use soft, thick mats for beds. People do not wear shoes in their homes.

Most South Koreans live in cities. They live in houses or apartments like those in North America.

Traditional homes have tile roofs. They have wooden walls and floors. People cover the floors with thick paper. The paper does not tear because people do not wear shoes. The homes have little furniture.

Ondol (ON-dol) floors warm South Korean homes. Hot water or air runs in pipes below ondol floors. Floors must be warm because some people eat and sleep there.

Some South Koreans live in apartments.

Going to School

South Korean children start school at age six. Students learn reading, writing, and math. They also study science, art, and music.

The government requires that students attend grade school for six years. Most students go to middle school for three years. Some students go on to three years of high school. Others learn job skills in trade schools. Some may attend college after high school.

South Korean students learn to write three different alphabets. People use the Han'gul (han-GUL) alphabet to spell Korean words. Students also learn to write in Chinese. South Koreans use the Chinese alphabet to write the names of people and places. Students learn the English alphabet in grade school. They study how to read and write English.

South Korean children start school at age six.

South Korean Food

Rice is an important food in South Korea. People eat rice at every meal. Rice usually is the main dish. Other parts of meals include vegetables, soups, fish, and meat.

South Koreans eat soup and stew. The Korean word for stew is chim (JEEM). Soup is kuk (KOOK). People make chim and kuk with vegetables, rice, and meat.

Kimch'i (kim-CHEE) is another common food in Korea. Kimch'i is a spicy, pickled vegetable dish. Many South Koreans eat kimch'i with every meal.

People traditionally sit on the floor at low tables to eat. Each person has a rice dish and a soup bowl. Other dishes are in the middle of the table. Everyone eats from these dishes. South Koreans use spoons and chopsticks to eat. Chopsticks are two thin pieces of wood.

South Koreans sit on the floor at low tables to eat.

South Korean Clothing

Everyday South Korean clothing is similar to clothing in North America and Europe. South Koreans wear traditional clothing on holidays and special occasions. South Koreans call their traditional clothing hanbok (HAN-boke). Hanbok is different for men and women.

Women wear ch'ima (CHEE-mah) and chogori (JUH-goh-ree). A ch'ima is a long skirt. A chogori is a short blouse. This clothing often is colorful.

Men wear paji (PAH-jee), turumagi (too-roo-MAH-gee), and chogori. Paji are long pants. Turumagi is a long coat. A man's chogori is a short jacket. Men wear turumagi over paji and chogori. Their clothing usually is white.

South Koreans wear traditional clothing on holidays.

Animals in South Korea

Many wild animals once lived in South Korea's forests. Goats and antelope made their homes there. Tigers, leopards, and sables lived there too. Sables are small animals with long bodies. They have short legs and soft fur.

People have destroyed much of South Korea's forests. Only small animals and birds live in the forests today. These animals include beavers, badgers, and rabbits.

Some deer live in the mountains and forests. Gorals (GOR-uhlz) also make their homes there. A goral is part goat and part antelope.

Cranes live in South Korea. These birds have long legs. Cranes wade in water to find food. Some cranes are white. White cranes are favorite birds of South Koreans. South Koreans believe these cranes stand for purity.

Gorals live in the mountains of South Korea.

Sports in South Korea

Tae kwon do (TEH KWON DOH) is a Korean martial art. A martial art is a style of fighting or self defense. Tae kwon do began in Korea more than 2,000 years ago. People all over the world practice tae kwon do today.

Ssirum (SEE-rum) is another Korean sport. It is similar to wrestling. People in Korea have practiced ssirum for 1,500 years.

South Koreans enjoy many other sports. People play soccer, baseball, tennis, and golf. Skiing, swimming, and basketball also are popular sports.

South Korea hosted the summer Olympic Games in 1988. The Olympic Games are sports contests among athletes from many nations. The Olympics took place in Seoul. South Koreans placed first in 12 events.

Tae kwon do is a Korean martial art.

Holidays in South Korea

South Koreans celebrate several national holidays. They have parties and go to events on these special occasions.

South Korea's New Year is in January. South Koreans call this holiday Sol. Families dress in their best clothes. They honor older family members. Families gather for large meals.

Children's Day is May 5. South Koreans honor children with parties on this day.

South Koreans celebrate Constitution Day on July 17. The government adopted the South Korean Constitution on July 17, 1948. The constitution set up South Korea's government.

South Koreans celebrate Ch'usok (CHU-sok) in August. Ch'usok is a harvest festival. People gather crops during harvest. Families get together for large meals on this holiday.

South Koreans honor children on Children's Day.

Hands on: Make a Mask

Masks are an important part of South Korean plays. Actors wear masks that match their characters. For example, happy characters wear masks with happy faces. You can make a mask.

What You Need

Paper plate	Tape	Glue	Construction paper
Craft stick	Markers	Scissors	

What You Do

1. Use the scissors to cut holes in the paper plate. You will need holes for eyes, a nose, and a mouth.
2. Make decorations for the mask with the construction paper. You can make a hat, a crown, or other shapes.
3. Glue the decorations onto the mask. Use the markers to color the mask.
4. Tape the craft stick to the bottom of the back of the mask. Craft sticks often come with frozen pops or ice cream treats. Hobby stores also sell craft sticks.
5. Hold the mask to your face with the craft stick. Now you have your own mask.

Learn to Speak Korean

excuse me	sille-hamnida	(SEE-leh-hahm-nee-dah)
good-bye	annyong	(AHN-nyung)
hello	annyong haseyo	(AHN-nyung hah-SEH-yoh)
no	anio	(AN-ee-oh)
please	put'ak hamnida	(POOT-ahk hahm-nee-dah)
thank you	kamsa-hamnida	(KAHM-sah-hahm-nee-dah)
yes	ye	(YEH)

Words to Know

chopsticks (CHOP-stiks)—two thin pieces of wood or metal used to eat

monsoon (mon-SOON)—a strong wind; monsoons can bring wet weather or dry weather.

peninsula (puh-NIN-suh-luh)—land surrounded by water on three sides

tradition (truh-DISH-uhn)—a belief, idea, or practice that people continue over many years; older people often teach traditions to younger people.

Read More

Jung, Sung-Hoon. *South Korea.* Economically Developing Countries. Austin, Tex.: Raintree Steck-Vaughn, 1997.

Ryan, Patrick. *South Korea.* Chanhassen, Minn.: Child's World, 1998.

Useful Addresses and Internet Sites

Embassy of the Republic of Korea
150 Boteler Street
Ottawa, Ontario K1N 5A6
Canada

Embassy of the Republic of Korea
2370 Massachusetts Avenue NW
Washington, DC 20008

Excite Travel: South Korea
http://city.net/countries/south_korea
Welcome to the Korean Embassy
http://korea.emb.washington.dc.us

Index